Ripe

poems by

Evelyn Ann Romano

Finishing Line Press
Georgetown, Kentucky

Ripe

Copyright © 2018 by Evelyn Ann Romano
ISBN 978-1-63534-677-0 First Edition
All rights reserved under International and Pan-American Copyright Conventions. No part of this book may be reproduced in any manner whatsoever without written permission from the publisher, except in the case of brief quotations embodied in critical articles and reviews.

ACKNOWLEDGMENTS

Thank you to the editors of these literary publications in which the following poems or earlier versions of them previously appeared.

Sandhill Review: "Sunday Morning Meditation"
Palm Prints: "Drought"
Hillsborough Cty. Lit Wit: "Ode to Summer Fruit"
Wordsmith: "What If", "Assigning Gender"
Bacopa Review: "Sisters of the Sea"
FSPA Anthology 32: "Clear"
New Mirage Quarterly: "Benign"
Palettes&Quills:Pencil Marks/ online: "Blindfolded"

Publisher: Leah Maines
Editor: Christen Kincaid
Cover Art: Katherine Michael
Author Photo: Simone Leal
Cover Design: Elizabeth Maines McCleavy

Printed in the USA on acid-free paper.
Order online: www.finishinglinepress.com
          also available on amazon.com

Author inquiries and mail orders:
Finishing Line Press
P. O. Box 1626
Georgetown, Kentucky 40324
U. S. A.

Table of Contents

Ripe 1

Sunday Morning Meditation 2

Drought 3

I Am 4

Swallowed 5

Family Gathering 6

Ode to Summer Fruit 7

Broken Warrior 9

Out of Order 10

What If 11

Muffin Pan on a Counter 12

At the Nursing Home 13

Benign 14

First Signs 15

Assigning Gender 16

Heat 17

Journey 18

Blindfolded 19

Sisters of the Sea 20

Yet 21

Rise Up, Soften 22

Clear 23

For my siblings: Jack, Barbara and Madelyn

Ripe

I awaken to find Eve.

Despite my pleading,
she refuses to enter.

Why does she resist
when I want to console?

Her focus is studied,
expression thoughtful:

*Expelled for a reason
I did not understand.*

*The garden was beauty,
its fruit fully ripe.*

*He never explained;
was I the victim?*

Come, take my hand.
I'll guide you home.

We'll begin again,
scatter lilacs in the sky.

Sunday Morning Meditation

Jogging down the path, I don't know
my body. My feet hit ground
but they step on clouds. The air
bonds with my breath. A heady scent

follows, feels like peace. Oaks and pines
are more than trees. My muse
is yellow warmth and the hug of blue
sky, the sigh of music from a solitary dove,
rabbits dashing to find safer space.

As I float, unaware of distance,
I see myself from the inside out
and throw open the doors I always
keep closed.

Drought

How do you scold
a half-dug pond
for its bumpy bottom,
feet of clay,

its head of cattail,
two-toned in greenish rust,
its slippery noon gaze
unmasking sweeps of muck?

At dusk a tiny ripple.
Birds swoop down
beaks wide open.
Palms and pines
indifferent partners.

I pray for rain.

I Am

a mardi gras
set free: a woman
banishing
my unobtrusive moon

sky
comforting the ground,
drawing, healing, becoming
a mountain

a clown
parading the stars
polishing bursts of
orange energy

a flower
caressing life
cultivating carnival
suns in heaven

Swallowed

the sun scribbles color
along the horizon
this day is over
without giving notice
light fades
in tiny steps
shadows a sweep of
haze: gray upon gray
a sea so pale
it disappears
this choreography
a model
i observe and dismiss:
i scurry around
get lost in the light
forget the dark
hold out my hands
swallow the wafer
darkness follows

Family Gathering

*A ripe tumult rumbles
in the belly.*
We sit so poised,
posed not for comfort
practiced preening
before an imaginary lens.
There is no lens, no matter,
shadow is substance
we perform out loud.
Lips stretch wide,
stay in place,
eager eyes
in starlet gaze:
*showy flowers
soften a snow.*
Conversation starts,
postures shift,
pretend attention:
birds in flight.
Words arise:
unholy offerings.
Lasting seconds
easily missed,
occasional lapse—
white fire.

Ode to Summer Fruit

Petulant, plush
velveteen suede
precious peach
of luscious shades.
Joyous bursts of juice,
sunsets let loose.

Kingdoms,
deep purples and blues,
keepers of the gate
of crush red and ooze.
Royal statesmen, sometimes glum
not always welcoming
ponderous plum.

Honeydew (not don't)
lacy, airy
light of sweetness.
Of moisture
droplets
fair-haired child
of sheen and clear
and my desire.

Orange madness
tight of skin
mapped for travel
dense within.
Fortress of pleasure
cant-a-loupe—
my sin.

Ovals and rounds,
greens and reds,
yellow-bellies
swallowed in beds.
Black slippery soldiers
invading the lush,
expelling the sweetness.
Oh, watermelon, yes!

Broken Warrior

Trash T.V. bellowed while I waited.
Harsh floors disabled light.
Voices hushed.

My husband lay deadened—
struggled to focus. Still supple
hair softened a graceless gurney.
Pink booties startled, his feet
made feminine.

His gown of daisies mocked solid
mass. Unknowing calves asserted
hope. A plastic bracelet flashed
age, name and gender,
as if this told something.

Shots of broken warriors picked
at my brain. I opened my purse,
fumbled for the pills. The valium
worked but I still felt helpless.

Thirty years together, we danced
out loud: the marathon runner,
Celtic dreamer. He promised to
stay strong. He was *so* very sure.

Now my lover, my partner, my
friend will walk with toes shuffling
the floor, hands grasping tightly
to a mechanical chair.

Out of Order

We rally around
order, demand that it
takes us. If we
lose order we lose ourselves:
Mother Nature lets go, quakes
the earth, a belly belch
of seismic spew; twisters slash
with quiet hum and oceans stretch
to swallow lives. We mourn

order's absence: failed
marriages, broken families, lost
children, all debris
traveling with shame.
Clouds, suns, and moons
all listen and love
their orderly commands,
else—God forbid!—they create
hell for humankind. So
Pluto, Earth, the voice inside
crave order, caress its needy beat,
worship at its feet. Do we

ever get sick of it? If
the television, the treadmill,
the ATM computer phone car
go out
of order
would we really wish
them back in?

What If

flowers

are us:

damaged and whole

jammed and free

noisy and still

blooming and dying.

Muffin Pan on a Counter

Soldiers, 12

in a row,

nipples erect,

sisters in action,

saluting sky.

Oh, how they

speak to me,

across a room.

At the Nursing Home

Dark brown hair, cut short, sets her apart
in a silver sea. A strong skilled arm
       lifts food to her mouth,
              she opens and swallows,
                     reflex not hunger.
She's wheeled back to her room and set
down to sleep. The sister I remember:

> *Hangin' on the corner encircled by boys, a
> teenage rebel dragged home by our father;
> popular cheerleader, star of the family, our
> mother's second self: long sweet hair, tiny
> chiseled bones, petite Celtic beauty. A 60's
> suffragette, a front lawn of signage: American
> Imperialism- Leave Vietnam. Her causes
> radical, always right. We traveled together and
> she took the lead. On beloved Irish soil she
> revealed her heart: " I look over my shoulder
> and you're always there. I'm afraid you'll catch up"
> I forced a half smile. She opened a bed and breakfast
> and graced the landscape of Dutchess County.
> Cinderella's life played out loud. Then the
> accident: a knockdown—darkness—*

I watch her sleep and the room turns alien. I check
the time and close my book. I leave her behind.

Benign

I collapse on the couch, gulp

ice cream, devour my novel.

Pleasure numbs me but I

strain for the cry of the phone.

Silence cleanses the midday air,

no respite from jumbled thought.

I choose to believe all is well.

For today, at least, I can.

Heat

Heat surrounds my body,
jumps inside
without giving notice
it exhales into gold:

I know a woman who lives forever and only drinks love.
She bottles stars and cries out-loud for Bonnie and Clyde.

She's airborne on sushi, surprises, sitar,
worships rivers, rainbows, cathedrals.

She is never confused by *what might have been.*

Wildflowers need passion to bloom through the weeds.

Blindfolded

Muscles harden, feet scatter,

heart scrambles. Do the blind

know more? I show form, chew fear,

taste presence. Must I breathe loss

to know *the other*? I claim love

as though the gods are mine alone.

I thank darkness that opens me.

Journey

Stars speak
in the dark
like dreams.
No one
listens. Matter
craves matter. No
shadow,
shade,
nuance.
We become
our dreams: shapeless
flowers, scented rivers,
grieving
muscle, Shiva's
dance, leaf
on a twig,
ant on a leaf
ambling along
unsure of edges
moving towards
home, wherever,
exactly, it is.
Throat
of the wind,
sun
we can't
touch.
Unknowable
yet real
as earth.
Actual
places, stars,
a journey
lead us
to us.

Assigning Gender

> *"Venice is the only city in the world which can never be confused with others"* ~Interpreti Veneziani

Venice walks into the
sea lifting her skirts:
long, long, legs
lacy black nylons
lacquered toenails
a wily smile
of fresh even teeth
to entice and bestow
black/blonde hair
stilted and showy
dripping with scent.
Italy's orphan,
Rome's embarrassment?

Venice commingles
 spilling out eggs
  wicked in water
  known on the streets
cantors cry for her
forecast her demise.

This woman is beautiful:

Heart kind as an angel's eyes.
Touch gentle as hands in prayer.
Light sacred as blessed candles.

The sea opens to receive her:

She is us, we are her.

First Signs
for my sister

Four board the vessel
amongst the crush,
two husbands, two wives,
adrift in Venezia.

They scramble for seats
but a wife is missing.
The husband races to the bow,
they return hand in hand.

Her bearing is bewildered,
startled surely. Now to the others:
" a simple wrong turn, you do understand?"

They smile on cue
but his eyes are crying.

Sisters of the Sea
Ireland's Cliffs of Moher

reaching out to nowhere
desperate to get there
never looking back
buried in cryptic secret, darkly crying
why do you weep, when you alone *exist?*

Mourning defines the air,
stills the sea. Skies disappear.
Grasses falter, can you not feel
their fear?

Rooted by bulk, the cliffs dare
not wade or dangle lest even
a twinge bares weakness. Softness
kills, my sullen sisters.

The cliffs' outstretched arms
reach to God and punish the sea.
A challenge, a test of might.
A need to match God as equals?

Sisters, hold tight, kiss the sea,
growl at approachers, caress
the Divine, never smile, embrace
stone, allow neither twist nor turn.

You are the entrance to the other side.

Yet

Open cartons release a life.

His sketches, plans and drawings
drop to the floor. Black ink, yellow paper
color the tile: houses, stores, malls
mingle in my home. They chat like
family in French, English and German.

I picture my uncle Bill, in a park perhaps,
in Paris or Kohl, inhaling a culture. No one
claims the cartons after he dies. They line
the baseboards of my writing room. I address
them often. Is the work
the man? If I trash his designs
does he die again?

Buildings live on in concrete and mortar.

Rise Up, Soften

Silver light cuts my bread,
windows draw

me out. Stillness rushes in, swells

on laden air. Table-top daisies
widen their smile, show more teeth.

Stools and chairs fall back
and lighten, ceilings and walls discard their seams.

Folk art paintings play their part, restate
their message, know they belong.

Floors rise up, soften, dissolve.

Cat, Aurora, slides into the light.

Clear

I wake,

find evil at the door,

bundled tight in a box,

smiling white, wide grins

that squeeze me back into dreams:

kaleidoscopic, zombie-like

clouds weaving through days, years

of clotted life: loss like a plunge to a

cavernous pit, like being lost

on the street where I live. Do they

mean what they say, these taunts,

flares of insight? Should I

clear them from my plate,

file as useless,

or pay attention?

The day outside is the same:

sun sneaking up, moist

warming air, singing

in the distance.

Words of Thanks

Heartfelt thanks and much gratitude to Katherine Riegel for her editorial review and suggestions for the manuscript. She has worked closely with me to make this chapbook a reality.

Sincere thanks to the members of the Ten O'Clock Poets for their insightful, supportive critiques: especially Cath Mason for her help with the final manuscript, as well as Simone Leal, Brenda Tipps, Morrey Grymes and the late "Bettie" Perez who I miss dearly. Also thanks to the wonderful friends who have supported and encouraged my writing from the beginning: Aileen Goding, Yvonne Duncan and Cindy Southers. I am also indebted to Lifelong Writers at the University of South Florida and the Tampa Writers Alliance for recognizing and publishing my poetry and offering me so many opportunities to garner awards and participate in readings.

Also many, many, thanks to Christen Kincaid and everyone at Finishing Line Press especially Leah Maines.

Lastly and most importantly thanks to my husband and soulmate, Albert whose love and support have made my journey possible.

Evelyn Ann Romano is a graduate of Rutgers University with a Bachelor of Arts in Psychology/English. Her poetry has been published in numerous journals and anthologies including *Bacopa Review, Sandhill Review, Wordsmith, Palm Prints, New Mirage Quarterly, Time of Singing, Palettes & Quills: Pencil Marks (online)* and *Florida State Poets Anthologies*.

She is a three-time Tampa Writers Alliance Poetry Prizewinner, including a first place win and publication for her poem, "Clear". She has won two awards for her poem, "Sisters of the Sea" by The Mount Dora Festival of Music and Literature and New River Poets. Her poem, "Ode to Summer Fruit" was a prizewinner in the Hillsborough County Library Lit Wit contest. She has participated in numerous poetry readings and loves sharing her work with an audience.

Aside from poetry, her other passion is Yoga. She has been practicing for many years and has attended Yoga Retreats in Costa Rica and Mexico. She has traveled widely in Europe and has a special place in her heart for Venice, Italy and her beloved Ireland.

A former Human Resources professional in New Jersey, she currently resides in Tampa, Florida with her husband Albert.

www.ingramcontent.com/pod-product-compliance
Lightning Source LLC
LaVergne TN
LVHW041519070426
835507LV00012B/1697